If It's to Be,
It's Up to Me!

If It's to Be,
It's Up to Me!

The ABC's of Character Building

Written and Illustrated by

Sally Snyder

ORANGE FRAZER PRESS

WILMINGTON, OHIO

ISBN 978-1933197-579

To order additional copies of *If It's to Be, It's Up to Me* or to make arrangements for the author to come to your school, please contact:

Sally Snyder
1341 Ironwood Court
Defiance, Ohio 43512
419.782.0778
http://sallysnyder.com

Printed in China

Library of Congress Control Number: 2008935548

This book is dedicated to all educators, parents, and grandparents who inspire their children to be the best that they can be.

Foreword

As we all know, growing up can be
challenging. Most of us have a strong
desire to "fit in" and to be accepted by our
peers. Sometimes that desire is so strong that
we make poor choices.

If It's to Be, It's Up to Me presents issues for discussion such as bullying, name-calling,
and spreading rumors. It also stresses the importance of having a positive attitude,
putting forth our best effort and accepting responsibility.

Speaking of responsibility, we all have an obligation to support and encourage our
children, while at the same time help them realize that making good choices and
decisions can lead to a lifetime of fulfillment and joy!

If It's to Be,
It's Up to Me!

Attitude begins with the letter A.

It's how we handle each day.

We can always argue and complain,

Or be cheerful and obey.

11

Bully begins with the letter B.

Bullies don't follow the rules.

They target others in word and deed.

It happens in most schools.

13

Clown begins with the letter C,

This word describes a child,

That always likes to entertain

And who can be quite wild.

c c c c c c c c c c c c c c c c c c c c c c c c c c c c c c c c c c c c c c c c c c c c c c c c c

15

Disappointed begins with

the letter D.

Your friends get an invitation.

Nothing happens to come your way,

And you see their jubilation!

d d d d d d d d d d d d d d d d d d d d d d d d d d d d d d d d

17

Effort begins with the letter E.

It's striving to do your best,

At home, school, work or play.

Are you up for the test?

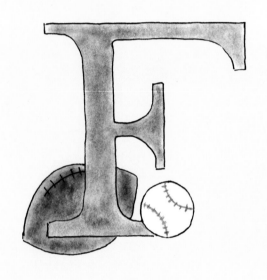

Friendship begins with the letter F.

It shows others that you care

By being there in times of need,

To listen, help, and share.

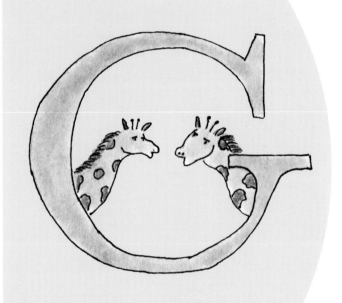

Gossip begins with the letter G.

People repeat a rumor.

They tell one person, then two.

It spreads and has no humor.

g g g g g g g g g g g g g g g g g g g g g g g g g g g g g g g g g g g g g g g g

23

Honesty begins with the letter H.

There's a very simple rule.

Tell the truth no matter what.

Your friends will think you're cool!

hhhhhhhhhhhhhhhhhhhhhhhhhhhhhhhhhhhhhhhhhhhhhhhhhhhhhh

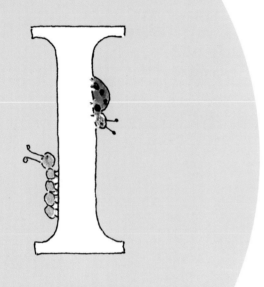

Individual begins with the letter I.

Every child is unique.

Regardless of the color of skin,

Respect is all they seek.

Jealousy begins with the letter J.

It's a feeling of envy and doubt.

Someone worked hard

to achieve a dream,

And others simply pout.

29

Knowledge begins with the letter K.

It's more than reading and math.

It's also learning right from wrong,

And choosing the very best path!

30

Love begins with the letter L.

It shows in everything you do,

Putting others before yourself,

Rewards will come back to you!

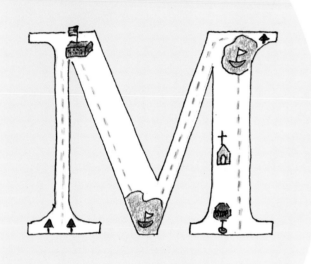

Manners begins with the letter M,

Say "excuse me" and "please,"

"Pardon me" and "thank you."

Kind words put others at ease.

34

35

Name-calling begins with the letter N,

Like four eyes, chubby and nerd.

You lower your image

when saying mean things.

Please...carefully choose each word.

Obstreperous begins

with the letter O,

When one is resisting and loud.

It's seeking attention in

negative ways,

Just to stand out in a crowd.

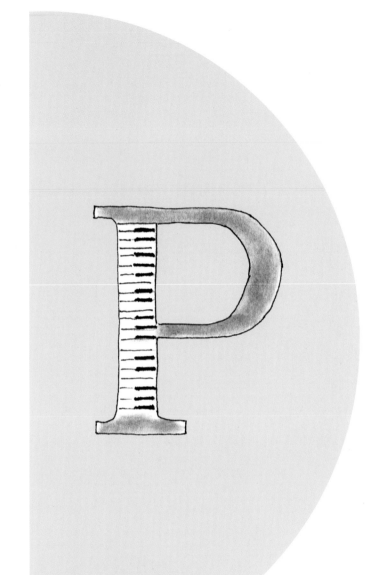

Persistence begins with the letter P.

It means to stay the course.

Set goals…work hard in all you do,

And you'll have no remorse.

ppppppppppppppppppppppppppppppppppppppppppppppppp

If you believe
in yourself
ANYTHING
is
POSSIBLE!

41

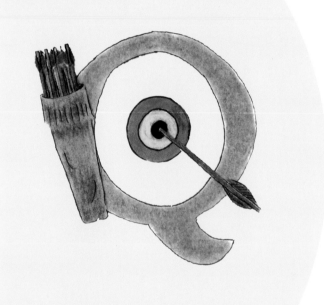

Quitting begins with the letter Q.

It happens when times get rough.

But instead of thinking of giving up,

Be strong, determined, and tough.

qqqqqqppppppppppppppppppqqqqqqqpppppppppppq

Responsibility begins

with the letter R.

It means to complete a task.

Whether the job is small or huge,

It's not too much to ask.

45

Sorry begins with the letter S.

Say it when you're wrong.

Swallow your pride and apologize,

You'll feel like singing a song!

47

Talent begins with the letter T,

Such as painting, singing, or dance.

With dedication and hard work,

There's an excellent chance

to advance!

49

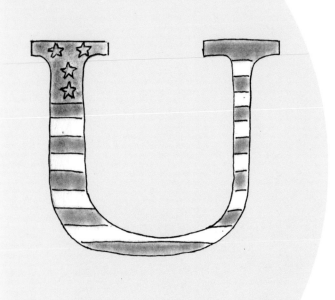

Understanding begins

with the letter U,

It also begins with me.

Reaching out to one another

We can change this world…

you'll see!

51

Volunteer begins with the letter V.

It's helping others in need,

Raking leaves, mowing grass,

Or teaching someone to read.

V V V V V V V V V V V V V V V V V V V V V V V V V V V V V V V V V V V V V V V V V V V V V V V V V V V V V V V V V V V V V

53

Welcome begins with the letter W.

A new student enters your school.

Step up and help him all you can.

Remember the Golden Rule?

Example is for the letter X.

Instead of following the crowd,

Stand up for what you believe in

And make the others proud!

X X X X X X X X X X X X X X X X X X X X X X X X X X X X X X X X X X X X X X X X X X X X X X X X X X X X X X X X X X X

Youth begins with the letter Y.

You're the future of our land.

Many problems will be solved,

By joining hand in hand!

Zest begins with the letter Z.

We know with living comes strife,

But if it's to be, it's up to me

To enjoy a zest for life!

z z z z z z z z z z z z z z z z z z z z z z z z z z z z z z z z z z z z z z z z z z z z z z z z z z z z z z z z z z z z z z z z

Glossary

Achieve ...... to do or to get with effort

Deed ..... a thing done; an act

Doubt ..... to be uncertain or undecided; to tend to disbelieve

Envy ..... desire for something that another person has

Image ...... how one person views another

Jubilation ..... a happy celebration

Knowledge ..... what is known; learning

Negative ..... not good; not as it should be

Obstreperous ..... noisy or unruly

Rumor ..... gossip; an unconfirmed report

Remorse ..... feeling guilt for one's actions

Target ..... to harm or hurt; victimize

Unique ..... one and only; special

Zest ..... enjoyment; happiness

About the Author

Sally Snyder grew up in the small town of Hicksville, Ohio. Upon graduation from high school, she attended Defiance College where she attained a B. S. Degree in Elementary Education.

After teaching for two years, she and her husband, Mike, started their family and Sally became a stay-at-home mom. Fourteen years and five moves later, (Mike was a teacher/coach) she reentered the teaching field and enjoyed the remainder of her career working with enthusiastic third graders! In 2003 she published her first book, *Hold the Fort*.

Sally has four grown children and six wonderful grandchildren. She lives in Defiance and enjoys gardening, writing, painting, playing golf and spending time with Mike and their little malti-poo, Molly!